Boldest Explorers

Stephanie Kim Gibson-Hardie

Series Editor
Jeffrey D. Wilhelm

Much thought, debate, and research went into choosing and ranking the 10 items in each book in this series. We realize that everyone has his or her own opinion of what is most significant, revolutionary, amazing, deadly, and so on. As you read, you may agree with our choices, or you may be surprised — and that's the way it should be!

T 4961

an imprint of

SCHOLASTIC

www.scholastic.com/librarypublishing

A Rubicon book published in association with Scholastic Inc.

Ru'bĭcon © 2007 Rubicon Publishing Inc.
www.rubiconpublishing.com

 is a trademark of The 10 Books

SCHOLASTIC and associated logos and designs are trademarks and/or registered trademarks of Scholastic Inc.

Associate Publishers: Kim Koh, Miriam Bardswich
Project Editor: Amy Land
Editor: Joyce Thian
Creative Director: Jennifer Drew
Project Manager/Designer: Jeanette MacLean
Graphic Designer: Deanna Bishop

The publisher gratefully acknowledges the following for permission to reprint copyrighted material in this book.

Every reasonable effort has been made to trace the owners of copyrighted material and to make due acknowledgment. Any errors or omissions drawn to our attention will be gladly rectified in future editions.

Cover: Explorer–© CORBIS

Library and Archives Canada Cataloguing in Publication

Gibson-Hardie, Stephanie Kim
    The 10 boldest explorers / Stephanie Kim Gibson-Hardie.

Includes index.
ISBN 978-1-55448-456-0

    1. Readers (Elementary) 2. Readers--Explorers. I. Title.
II. Title: Ten boldest explorers.

PE1117.G538 2007a   428.6   C2007-901982-X

1 2 3 4 5 6 7 8 9 10   10   16 15 14 13 12 11 10 09 08 07

Printed in Singapore

Contents

26

34

42

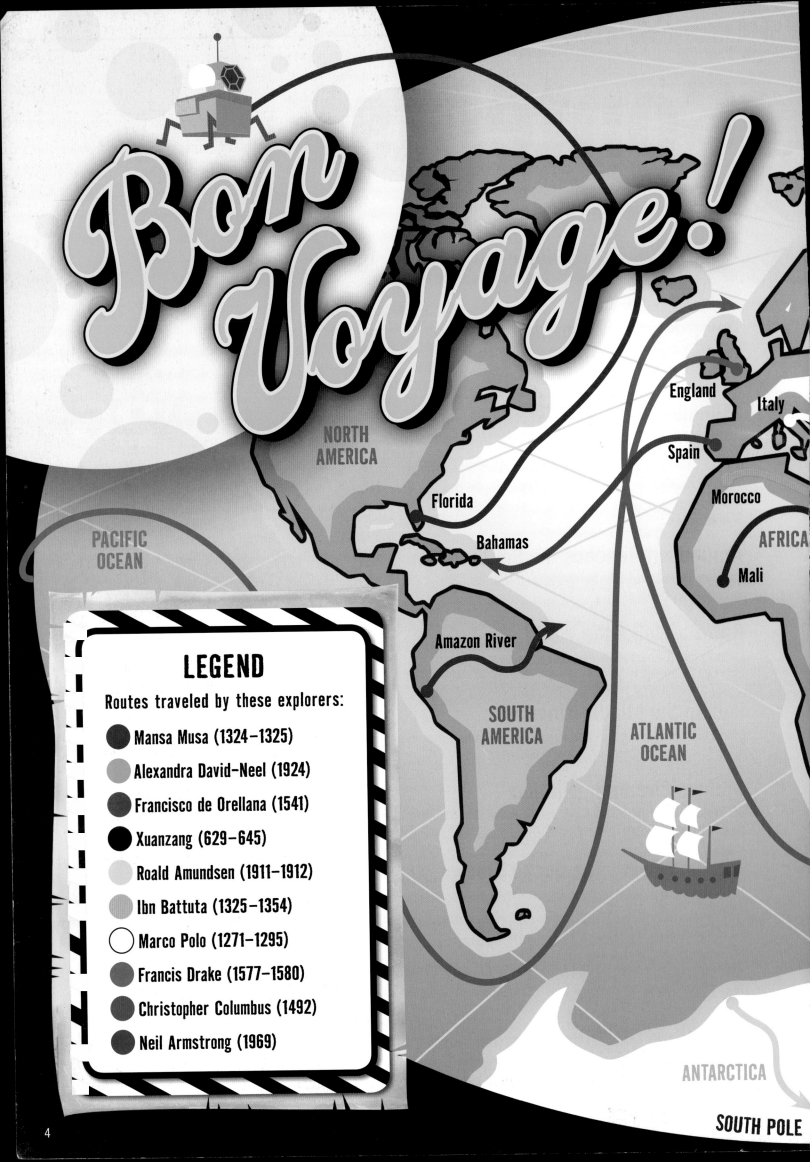

Bon Voyage!

NORTH AMERICA

PACIFIC OCEAN

Florida

Bahamas

Amazon River

SOUTH AMERICA

ATLANTIC OCEAN

England

Italy

Spain

Morocco

AFRICA

Mali

ANTARCTICA

SOUTH POLE

LEGEND

Routes traveled by these explorers:

- Mansa Musa (1324–1325)
- Alexandra David-Neel (1924)
- Francisco de Orellana (1541)
- Xuanzang (629–645)
- Roald Amundsen (1911–1912)
- Ibn Battuta (1325–1354)
- Marco Polo (1271–1295)
- Francis Drake (1577–1580)
- Christopher Columbus (1492)
- Neil Armstrong (1969)

ASIA

EUROPE

Lhasa

China

MIDDLE EAST

Mecca

India

PACIFIC OCEAN

How adventurous are you? Have you ever dreamed of visiting faraway lands, or exploring uncharted territory? If so, you're in good company!

For thousands of years, pioneers and adventurous people have crossed continents and oceans, traveling thousands of miles to faraway, sometimes forbidden lands. They were looking to explore places far beyond the known, in uncharted territories across the world and beyond. These journeys challenged the explorers' physical limits and tested their courage and determination. Some journeys even changed the course of history!

So what are you waiting for? The thrills begin as you start reading about who we think are the 10 boldest explorers in history.

Which of these explorers made the most amazing journey?

10 MUSA'S GOLD

Mansa Musa's journey to Mecca
brought fame and fortune to
him and his empire.

EN PILGRIMAGE

WHEN: 1324

THE ADVENTURER: Mansa Musa (? – 1337)

THE CHALLENGE: Make the trip from West Africa to Mecca with thousands in tow and lots of gold

In 1324, the great Egyptian city of Cairo was visited by an African king who was passing through on his way to the holy city of Mecca, in western Saudi Arabia. The city's historians would later record the event as one of the most amazing things to have happened that year. It's no surprise — Mansa Musa had a way of making great impressions.

Mansa Musa, the great Mali emperor, arrived in Cairo in style. More than 60,000 porters and 500 slaves were with him, each carrying a golden staff weighing six pounds. They were trailed by 80 camels, each hauling a package of gold dust weighing nearly 300 pounds. It was a golden parade of travelers, the likes of which the world had never seen.

Mansa Musa's journey was an exercise in generosity and kindness. Traveling across the Sahara, he gave fabulous gifts to everyone he met. His famous pilgrimage is one of the greatest recorded journeys in the history of the powerful western African kingdoms. Mansa Musa comes in at #10 on our list of boldest explorers.

---

porters: *attendants carrying baggage and other possessions*

MUSA'S GOLDEN PILGRIMAGE

GETTING PERSONAL

Mansa Musa is considered the most influential ruler of Mali. He was king from 1312 to 1337 — a time that is now called the "Golden Age" of Mali. He built the kingdom of Mali into an empire. His empire included most of western Africa.

WHY ON EARTH?

Mansa Musa was a devoted follower of Islam. Making the pilgrimage to Mecca (called a *hajj*) was a fulfillment of his duties as a Muslim. The journey was also an opportunity for the king to get to know the world outside of Mali. At the same time, he was determined to show off the greatness of his new empire.

Quick Fact

In total, Mansa Musa brought over two tons of gold on his journey. He used his gold nuggets and gold dust as a form of money. He also gave away a lot of this gold! As a result, gold became so common in Egypt that its value reportedly dropped significantly over the next decade.

DANGER AHEAD!

Crossing the Sahara to get to Mecca involved overcoming two obstacles: roaming robbers and lack of water. There was one other major worry for Mansa Musa. To go on this pilgrimage, he needed to leave his kingdom behind for more than a year! Being an absentee king could have posed a great danger to himself and Mali. But Mansa Musa trusted his Mali officials to keep order while he was gone.

AS A RESULT ...

Mansa Musa's journey brought him fame and prestige. Merchant cities in the Arab and European world began to take great interest in trading with Mali. Mansa Musa also returned with an Arabic library, scholars, and an architect who would later build great mosques and a royal palace in Mali. Largely because of Mansa Musa and his journey, the city of Timbuktu became a great center of African civilization.

Mansa Musa became the one and only African king to be pictured on European maps produced at the time.

The Expert Says...

"Mansa Musa's famous pilgrimage to Mecca in 1324 spread Mali's renown and prestige, not only in the Islamic countries but to the far corners of medieval Europe."

— Habeeb Salloum, travel writer

10   9   8   7   6

Preparing for the Pilgrimage

Mansa Musa's hajj would be no ordinary trek to Mecca. This account looks at the careful and thorough preparations that needed to be made to ensure the success of this journey:

Planning: Mansa Musa called on his most trusted elders to help him plan the details of his pilgrimage. The trip was to take no longer than 12 months (including stops in cities along the way, as well as the actual time Mansa Musa needed to spend in Mecca). They had to be smart and creative about planning their route — often, a longer route had to be chosen over a more direct route, because it was the only one with oases along the way.

Recruiting: Tens of thousands of people (including slaves, soldiers, and officials) were needed to beef up Mansa Musa's caravan.

Thankfully, Mali's young men and women were eager to volunteer — they knew it would be a great privilege to be part of the journey that would make Mali famous across the world.

Gathering Supplies: Besides the usual supplies of food and clothing, organizers also had to collect gold for Mansa Musa to use along the way. Provinces and trading towns throughout the Mali Empire were asked to do their part in helping pay for their king's journey.

? If you were a citizen of Mali, would you have supported paying for the trip? Explain your answer.

Securing Transportation: Organizers had a natural choice for their main mode of transportation: camels! For centuries, groups of travelers used camels as their pack animals. These animals were known for their endurance. They could go for several days without food and water while carrying extremely heavy loads and traveling long stretches.

Quick Fact
Wherever his caravan stopped for a rest, Mansa Musa paid for the construction of a new mosque.

Take Note
Many came before him and many have come after him, but no other pilgrim has ever matched the extravagance of Mansa Musa's journey to Mecca. For that, and for bringing unmatched fame and prestige to the empire of Mali, Mansa Musa comes in at #10 on our list.
- What do you think about Musa's decision, as leader of Mali, to leave his kingdom for a personal pilgrimage?

5   4   3   2   1

The Potala Palace symbolizes Tibetan Buddhism. It was built at an altitude of 12,100 feet in the center of Lhasa Valley, Tibet.

TREKS TO TIBET

WHEN: 1923 – 1924

THE ADVENTURER: Alexandra David-Neel (1868 – 1969)

THE CHALLENGE: Cross the Himalayas and slip into a forbidden city without getting caught

Ever since French traveler Alexandra David-Neel was a child, she had always wanted to leave the comfort of her home and set out for the unknown. "I dreamed of wild hills, immense deserted steppes and impassable landscapes of glaciers!" she wrote. Her curiosity and desire for freedom would lead her to amazing things.

At the age of 56, after years of traveling, David-Neel became the first foreign woman to enter Lhasa, the then-forbidden capital of Tibet, in central Asia. Countless other European adventurers had tried for centuries to catch a glimpse of this isolated place. Most failed or died trying. The only way to get to the "land of snow" was over the Himalaya Mountains — so that's exactly where David-Neel headed! She trekked her way across dizzyingly high mountain passes with her traveling companion, Aphur Yongden. They traveled under disguise and mostly at night. They had to, because if they had been discovered, it would have meant certain death.

In February 1924, David-Neel and Yongden arrived in Lhasa. The incredible journey they took, combined with the spirit of determination that led them through it, certainly earn David-Neel the #9 spot on our list …

steppes: *grass-covered fields found in southeast Europe, Siberia, and central North America*

"Adventure is the only reason for living," David-Neel once said. Do you agree? Explain your answer.

DAVID-NEEL TREKS TO TIBET

GETTING PERSONAL

Alexandra David-Neel was raised in a middle-class family. As a young girl, she preferred books on travel to dolls and dresses. At five, she escaped to explore a nearby forest, only to be dragged back home by a police officer. She traveled to England at 15, Switzerland at 17, and Spain at 18. In August 1911, she set sail for India and ended up staying in Asia for the next 14 years.

? Where in the world do you feel you must go in your lifetime, and why? What would you do if you encountered problems along the way?

WHY ON EARTH?

David-Neel journeyed to the holy city of Lhasa to soak up as much as she could of Tibetan Buddhism. Lhasa is the spiritual heart of the religion. She was able to find and bring back Buddhist texts no one outside of Tibet had seen before.

Buddhism: *a religion, founded in India by Gautama Buddha, which teaches discipline to overcome human desires*

DANGER AHEAD!

The route to Tibet that goes through the Himalayas was an unknown path — snow quickly covered any footprints or markings of a trail. Not only did the travelers have to cross high mountain passes, they had to face ferocious snow storms and icy weather. Cutting through the wilderness kept them safe from being discovered. But it also meant they had to find their own food and risk running into mountain bandits. David-Neel and Yongden once hiked for 19 hours straight, and went without food or water for more than 30 hours.

AS A RESULT ...

David-Neel's rare firsthand experiences made her Europe's leading expert on Tibet and Buddhism. She translated key Tibetan Buddhist texts, published numerous books (covering philosophy, geography, politics, and travel), and even gave lectures at universities. This laid the groundwork for many Europeans to discover Buddhist and Hindu philosophy.

This photo shows David-Neel dressed as a Tibetan nun.

Quick Fact

In 1912, David-Neel became the first European woman to meet the Dalai Lama, the spiritual and political head of Tibetan Buddhists. She met him while he was in India.

The Expert Says...

" The arduous voyage to Lhasa, the culmination of years of study and a familiarity with Tibet beyond the comprehension of most westerners, reduced David-Neel almost to a skeleton. "

— Barbara Foster, library sciences professor, City University of New York

arduous: *hard; exhausting*
culmination: *end*

10   **9**   7   6

Breathtaking

Crossing the Himalayas to get to Lhasa is a breathtaking trek in more ways than one! The city sits about 13,000 feet above sea level. On the altitude scale, this is considered "very high." Even if you aren't scared of heights, there are a number of other concerns facing the adventurer on such a climb. Here are instructions to follow for a safe climb!

1. **Beware of altitude illness!** If you go too high too fast, you might start feeling sick real quick. As you go higher up, the air becomes "thinner" — there's less oxygen in the atmosphere. This means you get less oxygen in your lungs with each breath, so the amount of oxygen in your blood declines (that is what makes you sick).

2. **Take it easy, but not too easy!** Once you get up to high altitude, light activity during the day is actually better than sleeping. That's because your breathing slows down during sleep — fewer breaths means even less oxygen than the low levels you're already getting.

3. **Two steps forward, one step back!** Once you start going above 10,000 feet, you should only climb 1,000 feet per day. You could climb more, but you'd actually need to come back down later to sleep at a lower altitude.

4. **Drink lots, eat lots!** Your body loses a lot more fluid than normal as you go up to high altitudes, so keeping hydrated is really important. You should also eat a high carbohydrate diet.

? How might these rules about climbing high altitudes have affected the progress of David-Neel's journey? There are many tips for climbing at high altitudes. Go online to find others not listed here!

Take Note

Unlike Mansa Musa at #10, David-Neel didn't have the privilege of traveling with a huge caravan of people to keep her company (or, more importantly, to keep her safe). Her journey is even more impressive when you consider the obstacles and attitudes she faced as a woman traveler of the late 19th century.
- Gender isn't the only barrier that can prevent someone from doing what he or she wants to do. What else can act as a barrier and why?

5   4   3   2   1

For more than eight months, Francisco de Orellana and his crew sailed the Amazon, one of the longest rivers in the world.

AMAZON RIVER–GETTY IMAGES

ILS THE AMAZON

WHEN: 1541

THE ADVENTURER: Francisco de Orellana (1490 – 1546)

THE CHALLENGE: Navigate the entire length of the mighty Amazon River, and stay alive!

Spanish explorer Francisco de Orellana had originally set out to discover gold and spices in the heart of South America. But a twist of fate brought him down one of the world's most powerful rivers.

Even today, a trip down the exotic Amazon River is a great adventure. In Orellana's time, it was an even more amazing expedition. Imagine sailing down a long, winding river through jungles full of strange and rare birds, monkeys, and other deadly beasts!

But Orellana took this on and became the first known European to sail the length of the mighty Amazon River. Read on to learn about this fantastic journey, and why Orellana ranks #8 on our list!

ORELLANA SAILS THE AMAZON

GETTING PERSONAL

Orellana was born in Trujillo, Spain. As a soldier, he joined Francisco Pizarro in Spain's takeover of Peru in 1535. This was Orellana's first taste of adventure into uncharted territories. He decided to join Pizarro's half brother, Gonzalo, in another expedition in 1538 — this time, to explore the interior of South America. It was this second exploration that led Orellana to the Amazon.

WHY ON EARTH?

Orellana and Gonzalo Pizarro originally set out to find new lands for Spain and gold in El Dorado, a mythical kingdom. But the men soon ran out of food and supplies. So Orellana sailed down the Amazon River to look for food. Here's where historians aren't sure what happened. Did Orellana sail all the way to the Atlantic Ocean because he couldn't return upstream against the river's strong current? Or did he continue on without the others so he could claim the glory for himself? (This is what Gonzalo Pizarro believed, as he felt he was left to die by Orellana.)

Sloths like to hang out in the jungle.

Quick Fact

As Orellana and Pizarro neared the Atlantic, their food consisted of iguana, monkey, sloth, and any fish they could catch. Do you think you would have been able to stomach these delicacies?

DANGER AHEAD!

The surrounding jungle, and the river itself, held many dangers. The Amazon is full of snakes (such as the anaconda), lizards, poisonous frogs, jaguars, and electric eels! Starvation was also a constant worry. At least seven men died from starvation.

AS A RESULT ...

Orellana's story of his adventure on the mighty Amazon brought the river worldwide attention. His reports also kick-started a series of exploratory voyages of the river and the many little streams that flow into it.

Boa constrictors are excellent tree climbers.

The Expert Says...

"[Orellana's] navigation and experience, which had been entered upon unintentionally ... turned out to be so extraordinary that it is one of the greatest things that ever happened to [humans]."

— Albert F. Kunze,
The Scientific Monthly

From El Dorado to Las Amazonas

Orellana's journey was documented in detail by a Dominican monk. In this account, the monk writes about what happened when Orellana made his way down the Amazon:

On the second day after we had set out and separated from our companions we were almost wrecked in the middle of the river because the boat struck a log ... if we had not been close to land we should have ended our journey there.

But matters were soon remedied thanks to the energy of the men in hauling the boat out of water and fastening a piece of plank on it, and we promptly started off on our way with very great haste.

As the river flowed fast, we proceeded on at the rate of 20 to 25 leagues, for now the river was high and its power increased ... We journeyed on for three days without finding any inhabited country at all. ...

leagues: *measure of distance that equals about 3 miles*
counsel: *advice*

[N]either on the next day nor on the following one was any food found, nor any sign of a settlement. ... [A]lthough we did wish to go back up the river, that was not possible on account of the heavy current, and there was no alternative, for to attempt to go by land was out of the question so that we were in great danger of death because of the great hunger we endured.

So, after taking counsel as to what should be done, talking over our affliction and hardships, it was decided that we should ... go forward and follow the river, and thus either die or see what there was along it. ...

? Orellana's decision to return for a second journey to the Amazon would ultimately lead to his death. Think of something in your life that you would be willing to take a huge risk for. Why do you consider it so important?

Quick Fact
To keep from starving to death, the travelers were forced to eat herbs stewed in horse blood that they cooked in their own helmets!

Francisco de Orellana

Take Note
David-Neel's journey into forbidden territory did require guts to follow through. But she had spent years preparing herself for her great journey. Francisco de Orellana did not have time to prepare. He sailed down the mighty river, but he still survived. That's why he comes in at #8.
• What other great discoveries, achievements, or inventions do you know of that were also "entered upon unintentionally"?

5   4   3   2   1

These ancient Buddhist carvings found in Hangzhou, China, date from the time of the pilgrim Xuanzang.

SACRED QUEST

WHEN: 629

THE ADVENTURER: Xuanzang (Shoo-ahn-dszang), 602 – 664

THE CHALLENGE: Make the trek from China to India through 118 different kingdoms to find the true Buddhist scriptures

When Xuanzang left his home to go on his quest, he was taking a big risk. It was the year 629. At the time, nobody was allowed to travel outside of the country — at least not without the emperor's permission. Even after being told not to go, Xuanzang left anyway, and headed straight for India.

Xuanzang was only 26 at the time. He was a well-recognized Buddhist monk and one of the most learned Buddhist scholars in China. Yet he longed for more. He dreamed of going to India, the birthplace of Buddhism, where he could collect ancient texts and study with master scholars. His fateful journey lasted about 18 years, and took him through some of the most rugged and dangerous land that separates China and India. He passed through great mountain ranges, vast deserts, and hundreds of foreign kingdoms. But in the end, he succeeded by accomplishing what many thought was impossible.

Xuanzang's deep personal conviction and undying faith gave him the strength to keep going. He comes in at #7 on our list of boldest explorers.

XUANZANG'S SACRED QUEST

GETTING PERSONAL

From the time he was a young boy, Xuanzang loved learning. Sometimes, he would study for hours without stopping to sleep or eat. He mastered the Buddhist scriptures at an early age. At 13, he officially became a Buddhist monk.

WHY ON EARTH?

Over time, Xuanzang began to notice problems with many of the Buddhist scriptures he was studying. He felt the Chinese translations were not so accurate. He believed that seeking the original texts was the only way to answer questions that troubled him and other Chinese Buddhists. This meant going to India, the birthplace of Buddhism. There, he would find the texts and the spiritual help he was looking for.

An illustration of Xuanzang from an ancient Chinese manuscript

Quick Fact

A king once tried to keep Xuanzang as a spiritual adviser. Xuanzang threatened to fast until he died. He was then released and he went back to India.

Buddhist prayer books

? Early on in his journey Xuanzang was abandoned by his companions and his guide. If you were him, how would you try to convince others to join you in your quest?

DANGER AHEAD!

Xuanzang had to cross deserts and climb mountains to get to India. On top of that, he had to travel at night — he couldn't let anyone see him because his journey was officially forbidden. As he continued on his journey, robbers tried to ambush him. Pirates nearly burned him at the stake, and even his guide tried to murder him!

AS A RESULT ...

Xuanzang's detailed writings about his journey provided China with the first reliable information about the different customs of surrounding kingdoms. More importantly, Xuanzang is recognized for his great contribution to the study and philosophy of Buddhism. On his return, he brought back 657 Buddhist texts. He spent the remaining years of his life translating 74 of these into more than a thousand volumes.

? Think of a time when you did something for the good of others, even though it didn't benefit you directly. Why did you do it?

10   9   8   **7**   6

Close Call

Xuanzang's disciple wrote a biography about him. It covered Xuanzang's entire life and included detailed accounts of his travels. This excerpt describes how Xuanzang almost died while crossing the Gobi desert in central Asia:

Then again, because of the winding character of the road, he did not know which way to follow .... [H]e thought thus within himself, "I made a vow at the first that if I did not succeed in reaching India I would never return a step to the East; what then am I now doing here? It is better to die in the attempt to go to the West, than to live by returning to the East." ...

boundless: *endless*
notwithstanding: *despite*

At this time [as he looked] in the four directions, the view was boundless; there were no traces either of man or horse, and in the night the demons and goblins raised fire-lights as many as the stars; ...

But notwithstanding all this his heart was unaffected by fear; but he suffered from want of water, and was so parched with thirst that he could no longer go forward. Thus for four nights and five days not a drop of water had he to wet his throat or mouth; his stomach was racked with a burning heat, and he was ... thoroughly exhausted.

From a biography about Xuanzang, translated by Samuel Beal (1911)

? The quest for knowledge is a powerful motivation. It has driven countless other explorers and adventurers in the course of history. What would happen if we suddenly lost the urge to find out more about ourselves and the world?

Quick Fact

Journey to the West, a popular Chinese folk novel written in the 16th century, was based on Xuanzang's travels.

The Expert Says...

" [There is a] growing appreciation of Xuanzang's indomitable spirit and extraordinary and unparalleled achievements. His real accomplishments, the richness of his legacy, the range of his influence, his eventual place in history will emerge in the fullness of time. "

— Sally Hovey Wriggins in *The Silk Road Journey With Xuanzang*

indomitable: *impossible to conquer*

Take Note

Xuanzang never once swayed from his goal. He set out to bring back the sacred scrolls and he didn't stop until he achieved this goal. For the strength of his conviction and the hardships he endured, he stands at #7.
• Xuanzang went against the wishes of his emperor to go on his journey. This decision could have cost him his life! What do you think of this decision? How would you justify going against the wishes of an authority figure?

5   4   3   2   1

Norwegian explorer Roald Amundsen pioneered an entirely new route to the South Pole and lived to tell about it.

HES THE SOUTH POLE

WHEN: 1911

THE ADVENTURER: Roald Amundsen (1872 – 1928)

THE CHALLENGE: Start from the Arctic and be the first person to make it to the South Pole on the other side of the world!

There's no better example of the bold Viking spirit of adventure than Roald Amundsen. The Norwegian explorer devoted his life to exploring the icy polar regions of our planet. And it all paid off in 1911.

After crossing the Northwest Passage, Amundsen turned his sights to what would be his most famous journey: a bold expedition to become the first person to reach the South Pole. Amundsen and his crew completed the almost 1,900-mile trek in 99 days. It was a monumental achievement, not only to reach his final destination, but to return safely. His competitor, a British explorer by the name of Robert F. Scott, was not so lucky. Scott and his team died before making the trip home. For reaching the ends of the Earth, Roald Amundsen's landmark journey earns him the #6 spot on our list.

Northwest Passage: a sea route through the Canadian Arctic

Do you think having a competitor gives us a harder push to succeed? Or does it only result in "unsportsmanlike" behavior? Explain your answer.

AMUNDSEN REACHES THE SOUTH POLE

GETTING PERSONAL

When Amundsen was just 14, his father died and his brothers left home. His mother was the only family he had left. So when she said she wanted him to become a doctor, he did as he was told. But when she died, Amundsen dropped out of medical school right away. His true passion had never been medicine — he wanted to be an explorer! As a young boy, he even slept with the windows open — he said the icy Norwegian air would help prepare him for a future in polar exploration.

WHY ON EARTH?

Amundsen's original goal was to reach the North Pole. His plans were shattered in April 1909 when he heard that another explorer had beaten him to it. So Amundsen reversed directions — he decided he would become the first person to reach the South Pole!

DANGER AHEAD!

To get to the South Pole, Amundsen and his team had to withstand the fierce forces of nature. What did they expect — they were going through one of the harshest landscapes on Earth! During their expedition, they faced blinding blizzards, freezing temperatures, and gigantic glaciers. They often had to make their way across great ice crevasses (one wrong step and they would have fallen to their deaths!). Although they brought food and supplies, they still nearly starved to death.

AS A RESULT ...

Amundsen was the first person to go to both the South Pole and the North Pole in one lifetime! Not only was his journey to the South Pole incredibly daring, it also helped contribute to the scientific community. He came back with a wealth of valuable data about Earth's magnetism.

Amundsen relied on trusty huskies called Greenland dogs to pull his sleds.

Quick Fact

When he made his trip through the Northwest Passage in the Canadian Arctic in 1903, Amundsen became closely acquainted with an isolated Inuit tribe, the Netsilik. He used their dog sleds, slept in their igloos, and even wore their reindeer fur clothes.

? Living and learning from an Inuit tribe was a key factor behind Amundsen's success. What can we all learn from other cultural groups? Give examples.

10   9   8   7   **6**

The Day I Reached the Pole

Roald Amundsen kept a journal in which he wrote about his daily experiences during his expedition. Here is his personal account describing the day he reached his goal. He and his team arrived at the South Pole, at 3:00 PM on December 14, 1911.

The goal was reached, the journey ended. I cannot say — though I know it would sound much more effective — that the object of my life was attained. …

The regions around the North Pole — well, yes, the North Pole itself — had attracted me from childhood, and here I was at the South Pole. Can anything more topsy-turvy be imagined?

? Why would achieving a goal as huge as reaching the South Pole make him feel "topsy-turvy"?

We reckoned now that we were at the Pole. Of course, every one of us knew that we were not standing on the absolute spot; it would be an impossibility with the time and the instruments at our disposal to ascertain that exact spot. But we were so near it that the few miles which possibly separated us from it could not be of the slightest importance. …

Roald Amundsen

After this we proceeded to the greatest and most solemn act of the whole journey — the planting of our flag. Pride and affection shone in the five pairs of eyes that gazed upon the flag, as it unfurled itself with a sharp crack, and waved over the Pole. …

I had determined that the act of planting it — the historic event — should be equally divided among us all. It was not for one man to do this; it was for all who had staked their lives in the struggle, and held together through thick and thin. This was the only way in which I could show my gratitude to my comrades in this desolate spot. I could see that they understood and accepted it in the spirit in which it was offered. Five weather-beaten, frost-bitten fists they were that grasped the pole, raised the waving flag in the air, and planted it as the first at the geographical South Pole. …

From The South Pole: An Account of the Norwegian Antarctic Expedition in the 'Fram,' 1910 – 1912 *by Roald Amundsen*

The Expert Says…

" [Amundsen's journey was] a victory of human mind and human strength over the dominion and powers of Nature; a deed that lifts us above the gray monotony of daily life … the triumph of the living over the stiffened realm of death. "

— Fridtjof Nansen, Norwegian explorer, scientist, and diplomat

dominion: *area of control*

Take Note

Xuanzang at #7 had to trek for many years, but he didn't have to face the harshest climate on Earth! For being the first person to ever reach the elusive South Pole and with all the forces of nature against him, Amundsen earns the #6 spot on this list.

• Think back to a time when you wanted to do something you were told was impossible. How did that make you feel — did it motivate you more or put a damper on your plans?

Battuta is the only medieval traveler known to have visited the lands of every Muslim ruler of his time.

ARAB NOMAD–ISTOCKPHOTO

KS THE WORLD

WHEN: 1325

THE ADVENTURER: Abu Abdallah Ibn Battuta (1304 – 1368)

THE CHALLENGE: Travel alone around the world, going from Morocco to Northern Africa, the Middle East, India, and Central and East Asia

In 1325, 21-year-old Abu Abdallah Ibn Battuta set out for Mecca from Morocco. He had decided go on this religious journey despite all the challenges he knew he would have to face.

First, he crossed North Africa. He set out alone and traveled slowly, going by foot, horse, donkey, or camel. Eventually, he joined a caravan of hundreds (some say thousands) of other pilgrims heading toward Mecca. After months of touring through the Middle East, he finally arrived at the holy city in 1326.

Like Musa at #10, Battuta completed a hajj. However, he made a decision that would change his life forever. Instead of going home, he pressed on, going North, South, East, and West to see more places and meet more people. In the end, he stayed on the road for 29 years and covered more than 75,000 miles!

When Battuta finally returned home, his whole world had changed. He had become a worldly, middle-aged man, soon to be famous for his travels. The record of Battuta's journey would go down in history as perhaps the greatest travel essay ever written. He comes in at #5 on our list …

Do you think you could travel for 29 years like Battuta? Think about the places you could see, but also consider what you might miss back home.

BATTUTA WALKS THE WORLD

Quick Fact

His longest stay in one city was in Delhi, India, where he spent eight years serving the sultan as a qadi, or judge. The sultan himself then sent him onward to China as his personal ambassador.

GETTING PERSONAL

Battuta was born in Tangier, Morocco. His parents were both Muslim scholars who studied religious law. Taking after his parents, Battuta studied religious texts, poetry, and legal sciences. Legend says he had an amazing memory. This would help him later in life when he had to tell the tale of his incredible journey upon his return home.

WHY ON EARTH?

Battuta's original reason for leaving his home was to make a holy pilgrimage to Mecca. What was his reason for staying on the road another 29 years? He had a major thirst for knowledge! He wanted to know more about the world around him, to meet new people, and to learn about different cultures. This was why he made multiple pilgrimages to Mecca and continued traveling until he felt ready to return home.

Today, we can travel great distances in just a few hours, unlike the months and years it took for a traveler like Battuta. Do you think the modern traveler could do what Battuta did? What do you think we would miss by going from one place to another so quickly?

DANGER AHEAD!

Battuta always chose the least-traveled paths. He also took many detours along the way. During his 29 years on the road, he went through it all — he was attacked by bandits, he got shipwrecked and lost all his belongings, and he was almost beheaded by a tyrant ruler. When he finally tired of all the drama on the road, he made his way back to Morocco — and came face-to-face with the black plague! Thousands were dying from the disease in the towns he passed through, but he escaped without catching it.

AS A RESULT ...

Battuta went on his worldwide travels to learn more for himself. But thanks to his book about his travels, *Rihla*, he was able to share what he saw and heard in parts of the world many people didn't even know existed. At the time, Battuta's descriptions of these little-known places (including the religious, political, and social conditions there) were the only glimpses the Western world had into Eastern civilization.

Battuta traveled on camel for most of his journey.

The Expert Says...

"Ibn Battuta, who traveled farther than any writer before him, is rightly considered one of the great medieval voyagers ..."

— Michael Wolfe in *One Thousand Roads to Mecca: Ten Centuries of Travelers Writing About the Muslim Pilgrimage*

10   9   8   7   6

IN HIS OWN WORDS

It should be no surprise that Battuta had his share of ups and downs during his journey. In these quotations from Battuta's book, *Rihla*, he tells us how he felt during some of the toughest moments of his journey:

Traveling alone:

"I felt so sad at heart on account of my loneliness that I could not restrain the tears that started to my eye, and wept bitterly. But one of the pilgrims, realizing the cause of my distress, came up to me with a greeting and friendly welcome, and continued to comfort me with friendly talk until I entered the city. ..."

Leaving home:

"I set out alone having neither fellow-traveler in whose companionship I might find cheer, nor caravan whose party I might join, but swayed by an overmastering impulse within me and a desire long-cherished in my bosom to visit [Mecca]. So I braced my resolution to quit all my dear ones ... My parents being yet in the bonds of life, it weighed sorely upon me to part from them... ."

braced: *strengthened*

Returning home:

"I was moved [to go back] by memories of my homeland, affection for my family and dear friends, who drew me toward my land, which, in my opinion, was better than any other country."

? If you should feel homesick when traveling, what could you do to feel better?

Take Note

Like Amundsen at #6, Battuta had to rely on the kindness of strangers to help him throughout his journey. But unlike Amundsen, Battuta stayed on the road for 29 years and went through multiple different environments. He didn't make any special preparations either.
• Think of what you would need to go from one environment to another. How would you prepare for different climates and terrain?

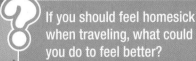

A 14th century painting of Marco Polo and his father and uncle leaving Venice

WHEN: 1271

THE ADVENTURER: Marco Polo (1254 – 1324)

THE CHALLENGE: Travel throughout the Middle Kingdom (ancient China) and visit places he'd never seen before

The world was a very different place in the 13th century. Merchants and explorers were some of the most important people of the day. And they were obsessed with finding trade routes that would lead them to riches and fame.

Marco Polo just happened to be the son and nephew of two trailblazing merchants and explorers from Italy. He followed in their footsteps and became an outstanding explorer, too. But his adventurous heart led him one step further. He journeyed to the far reaches of Asia and continued traveling throughout the entire Middle Kingdom.

By the time Polo returned to his home in Venice, Italy, in 1295, he had been on the road for 24 years! He'd visited places many of his fellow Europeans had never even heard of and seen things they could hardly imagine. His journey of discovery and exploration lands him at #4 …

POLO IN THE MIDDLE KINGDOM

GETTING PERSONAL

Marco Polo was born into a wealthy merchant family. His father and uncle were both experienced travelers because of their work — and they took young Polo out east. Polo had always been interested in different cultures and peoples, as well as exotic plants and animals.

WHY ON EARTH?

On their earlier journeys, the two older Polos had made friends with the great Kublai Khan, emperor of the Mongol Empire. When they returned with Polo in 1271, the young man made quite the impression on Khan with his strange tales of their travels. That was when Khan decided to send Marco Polo out to distant parts of the empire. Polo's mission: to find out as much as he could and bring back more stories of different practices and peoples in the rest of China.

DANGER AHEAD!

Marco Polo passed through many foreign lands during his journey. He crossed extremely dry deserts infested with bandits. These thieves robbed merchants and diplomats who often carried lots of riches on their travels. Besides this, Polo also had a long fight with an illness (possibly malaria). On his return to Italy, he ran into monsoon season. The extreme weather forced his party to stop over for almost half a year to avoid getting shipwrecked.

AS A RESULT ...

Everything Polo saw, or heard, or read about while on the road went into his book, *Il Milione* (known in English as *Travels of Marco Polo*). Interest in exploration and mapmaking exploded after it came out. It also became somewhat of a guidebook for merchants and diplomats on how to do business with the Mongol Empire. It was Polo's stories that inspired another famous explorer, Christopher Columbus, to set out to find the riches and luxuries of Asia.

Quick Fact

After he returned from his journey, Polo stayed in Venice until his death in 1324. On his deathbed, he is famously believed to have said: "I have only told the half of what I saw!"

Marco Polo and his father meeting Kublai Khan

10   9   8   7   6

Lost in the Desert

Marco Polo's Il Milione *wasn't just a guidebook for merchants. It doubled as a true adventure tale! This book excerpt gives us a look at the chilling side of being on the road:*

When a man is riding through this desert by night and for some reason — falling asleep or anything else — he gets separated from his companions and wants to rejoin them, he hears voices talking to him as if they were his companions, sometimes even calling him by name.

Often these voices lure him away from the path and he never finds it again, and many travelers have got lost and died because of this. Sometimes in the night, travelers hear a noise like the clatter of a great company of riders away from the road; if they believe that these are some of their own company and

head for the noise, they find themselves in deep trouble when daylight comes and they realize their mistake. ...

Even by daylight men hear these voices, and often you fancy you are listening to the strains of many instruments, especially drums, and the clash of arms.

For this reason bands of travelers make a point of keeping very close together.

Before they go to sleep they set up a sign pointing in the direction in which they have to travel, and round the necks of all their beasts they fasten little bells, so that by listening to the sound they may prevent them from straying off the path.

? Marco Polo stayed on the road for 24 years. Do you think you could have done this — going from place to place for years on end with no permanent home? Why or why not?

The Expert Says...

" Consider only what a height of courage was needed to undertake and carry through so difficult an enterprise, over a route of such desperate length and hardship ... not for days only but for months together. "

— Giovanni Battista Ramusio, 16th century Italian geographer

Take Note

Both Battuta and Polo spent an amazingly long time on the road. Polo's journey stands out more because he ventured beyond his comfort zone and into completely foreign places. Battuta traveled mostly to parts of the Islamic world where he expected hospitality from his fellow Muslims. That's why Polo edges out Battuta to take the #4 spot on our list.

• If you were an ambassador for the United States, where would you want to go? What would you hope to accomplish?

5 **4** 3 2 1

Drake set sail in 1577 and did not return home until 1580.

CUMNAVIGATION

WHEN: 1577

THE ADVENTURER: Francis Drake (? – 1596)

THE CHALLENGE: Take to the seas, dare to face the powerful Spanish Empire, and make it back home to England by sailing around the world!

Francis Drake didn't shy away from anyone or anything. That made him one of the most courageous as well as controversial sea captains of his time. But his story is also marked by a shining achievement.

At a time of great rivalry between the powerful Spanish Empire and an increasingly powerful England, Drake was sent on an expedition. Drake's mission — backed by Queen Elizabeth I — was to show the Spaniards what England was capable of. So he sailed from England to South America where the Spaniards were beginning to build an empire of colonies. There, he attacked and robbed the Spanish-controlled coast. Then he made a run for it! By the time he returned to England, Drake was hailed as the first from his country to sail around the world!

This circumnavigation of the world goes down as one of the most difficult and daring journeys of all time. And that's precisely why Drake comes in at #3 on our list.

DRAKE'S CIRCUMNAVIGATION

GETTING PERSONAL

As a young teenager, Francis Drake was forced to move closer to the coast of England with his family. If they hadn't moved, he probably would have become a farmer! In his new surroundings, young Drake quickly became an apprentice to an elderly sea master. At 13, he learned how to sail. Drake stayed close to England until his early 20s, when he began to sail with an Atlantic fleet. He made a name for himself during voyages to the West Indies.

WHY ON EARTH?

Queen Elizabeth I couldn't stand to watch her country's rival, Spain, build a vast empire across the ocean. In 1577, she sent Drake on a mission to go west and attack Spanish ports and treasure ships in the Pacific Ocean. This worked out perfectly for Drake — he had always wanted to make the Spaniards pay for robbing him on his earlier voyages. Besides this, Drake had other goals in mind: treasure, adventure, and fame!

DANGER AHEAD!

Drake hadn't gotten very far before his crew threatened to kill him and end the journey. He crushed the mutiny and carried on the journey with fewer men. Then, Drake had to watch out for the Spaniards as they neared South America. Along the way, illness and tropical diseases threatened to sideline the mission. A series of storms and hurricanes that lasted more than a month even destroyed one of the ships. Things got more dangerous on the return journey — Drake's ship, the *Golden Hind*, could barely sail under the weight of all the stolen loot captured from the Spanish. By the time they got back to England, only 56 of Drake's original crew of 100 remained.

AS A RESULT ...

Drake's descriptions of what he saw gave Europeans a more accurate picture of what the world was like across the ocean. His success was a victory for England — now recognized as the stronger power at sea.

? Imagine that your government wanted to send you on a similar mission — would you go? Why or why not?

Quick Fact

Drake's logbook and charts from his journey were hidden away by Queen Elizabeth I in 1580. She was afraid Spain would build up their army against the British Navy if they found out about Drake's route.

The knighting of Sir Francis Drake by Queen Elizabeth I in 1581

The Expert Says...

"[Drake] was the real founder of generations of seamen, and his undying fame will inspire generations yet unborn to maintain the supremacy of the seas."

— Walter Runciman in *Drake, Nelson and Napoleon*

THE GOLDEN HIND

Drake originally set out on his journey with five ships.
Only the *Golden Hind* completed the journey around the world.
Check out the details in this fact chart.

The Golden Hind *was originally named the* HMS *Pelican.*

MEASUREMENTS

The *Golden Hind* was a warship — a multi-decked sailing ship called a "galleon." It was about 70 feet long, 19 feet wide, and 9 feet deep. It weighed about 100 tons and had 18 small cannons. Historians say these measurements actually made it rather puny for a ship that was about to venture into enemy waters!

ONBOARD

Besides the seamen and officers in the crew, there were soldiers, gentlemen-adventurers, a shoemaker, a tailor, and musicians to play during dinner. Drake's brothers and uncles came along for the trip, too!

BUILD

The hull (body of the ship) was made of two layers of oak wood with sheets of lead between the layers. The cabins were finely furnished with carved oak tables and chairs, silk cushions, and silver plates. Not too shabby!

DISTINCTIONS

Drake was knighted "Sir Francis Drake" aboard the *Golden Hind* by Queen Elizabeth I in 1581. Between 1968 and 1970, Great Britain had a stamp featuring the legendary ship.

Take Note

Polo's Kublai Khan-backed adventures were tame compared to Drake's pirate battles on the high seas! Drake's daring adventures not only changed his fortunes, but those of England as well! This earns him the #3 spot on our list.
• What motivated Drake to go on his mission? Compare him to another explorer in this book.

5   4   **3**   2   1

This illustration shows Christopher Columbus approaching the coast of Bahamas in his dinghy. His ship is in the distance.

LS THE OCEAN BLUE

WHEN: 1492

THE ADVENTURER: Christopher Columbus (1451 – 1506)

THE CHALLENGE: Dare to sail into the unknown!

In 1492, Christopher Columbus set sail from Spain for his first of four voyages into the Atlantic Ocean. It was a big deal to venture into the Sea of Darkness, as the Atlantic was called at the time. Little did Columbus know that by sailing into the unknown, he was gliding right into the history books!

Columbus and his crew really didn't know where they were headed. And they had no accurate maps telling them what lay ahead. For 10 weeks they sailed farther and farther southwest until one night they finally spotted land. Columbus thought he'd found Asia. But of course he hadn't. No, he'd found new continents he didn't even know were there — the Americas. Columbus inadvertently became the connection between the Old World and the New World, and the rest, as they say, was history.

When he returned to Spain, his royal rulers named him the "Admiral of the Ocean Seas." For daring to brave the unknown, this determined sea captain takes the #2 spot on our list of boldest explorers.

 If you were to explore unknown territory — land or water — how would you keep track of where you were?

COLUMBUS SAILS THE OCEAN BLUE

GETTING PERSONAL

Columbus was born in the port city of Genoa, Italy, and later moved to Savona. He grew up surrounded by great ships and adventurous sailors. His love for the seas led him to pursue work aboard various ships (including one job as a pirate!). He eventually moved to Portugal — a leader in exploration at the time.

WHY ON EARTH?

For the longest time, European explorers and traders took the same route to get to Asia — sailing east across the Mediterranean Sea and then traveling by caravan across deserts and mountains. This was a long and troublesome route, so many explorers dreamed of finding a direct sea route. The Portuguese tried sailing all the way around Africa and then across the Indian Ocean. Columbus, on the other hand, was determined to get to the East by going westward. Some people thought the world was flat, but the promise of honor and wealth in the form of gold, jewels, and spices was too attractive.

DANGER AHEAD!

As if sailing into uncharted territories wasn't scary enough, Columbus had to worry about the possibility of not being able to get back home. Wind kept pushing them farther and farther southwest. Columbus's crew thought they'd never be able to sail back home against the strong winds. They were also constantly afraid they'd run out of food. Then there were the storms, which either blew Columbus off course or forced his ship ashore (smashing it to pieces).

Quick Fact

Returning from his first voyage, Columbus ran into a ferocious storm. It was so bad that he thought he wasn't going to make it, so he wrote up an account of his discoveries, sealed it in a barrel, and tossed the barrel overboard!

AS A RESULT ...

Columbus's "discovery" of the New World resulted in centuries of European colonialism in the Americas. Life changed forever on both sides of the Atlantic after this. For nearly 500 years, other explorers used Columbus's route to get from the Old World to the New World.

? What part would you say Columbus played in the history of colonialism in the Americas? With this in mind, how do you think historians should treat the subject of Columbus and his journeys?

Columbus's 1492 voyage to the Americas

Quick Fact

Many of Columbus's crewmen still believed the world was flat. They thought the ocean might boil once they reached "the ends of the Earth"!

10   9   8   7   6

Versus
COLUMBUS COLUMBUS

Not everyone has the same opinion about Christopher Columbus's four voyages to the Americas. Here's a look at two opinion pieces about the admiral's contribution to history:

"It's easy enough to be cynical about him nowadays. ... Yet in the broad sweep of history, most scholars agree, Columbus is a figure of unique importance. If his landing on American soil was not the first by a European ... it was the most decisive. It marked the beginning of sustained contact between the Old World and the New — the beginning, really, of the world we know."

— David Gelman, *Newsweek*

"After he failed to contact the emperor of China, the traders of India, or the merchants of Japan, Columbus decided to pay for his voyage in the one important commodity he had found in ample supply — human lives. ... Onboard Columbus's slave ships, hundreds died; the sailors tossed the Indian bodies into the Atlantic ... the first casualties of the holocaust of American Indians. ...

— Dr. Jack Weatherford, professor of anthropology, Macalester College

Christopher Columbus

The Expert Says...

"Other explorers sailed farther, suffered greater hardships, faced greater dangers and discovered more extensive coastlines; but few journeys have had such immediate and important consequences as those of Columbus."

— Ian Cameron in *Explorers & Exploration*

Take Note

Drake at #3 made his way around the world, but the historical impact of Columbus's journeys is undeniable. It changed the way people saw the world forever.

• Considering all the controversy surrounding Columbus's journey, do you think he deserves the #2 spot on our list? Why or why not?

5   4   3   **2**   1

Neil Armstrong, mission commander of Apollo 11, was the first man to step off the Lunar Module and walk on the moon.

NEIL ARMSTRONG & MOON SURFACE-NASA

ANDS ON THE MOON

WHEN: 1969

THE ADVENTURER: Neil Armstrong (1930 –)

THE CHALLENGE: Blast off from the Kennedy Space Center in Florida, toward the moon — a journey never made before

On July 16, 1969, hundreds of millions of people were glued to their TV sets. They watched as *Apollo 11* blasted off toward the final frontier … the moon!

Six and a half hours after landing on the lunar surface, American astronaut Neil Armstrong descended from the Lunar Module. His first words were: "That's one small step for [a] man, one giant leap for mankind." Armstrong's second in command, Buzz Aldrin, joined him and announced, "Beautiful. Beautiful. Magnificent desolation."

The journey to the moon and back took eight days to complete. The astronauts traveled more than 600,000 miles! The mission fulfilled President John F. Kennedy's goal of landing a man on the moon and returning him safely to Earth by the end of the 1960s. *Apollo 11*'s mission commander, Neil Armstrong, blasts into the #1 spot on our list.

desolation: lifeless emptiness

ARMSTRONG LANDS ON THE MOON

Quick Fact

Many of the people at NASA thought the *Apollo 11* astronauts might not return safely to Earth. President Richard Nixon even had a special backup speech in case of a terrible tragedy.

GETTING PERSONAL

Neil Armstrong had always wanted to fly since he was a young boy. At 20, he was the youngest pilot in his squadron. He had the rare opportunity to be the commander of the *Apollo 11* mission to the moon in 1969. He was joined by Edwin "Buzz" Aldrin, lunar module pilot, and Michael Collins, command module pilot.

? In the 1950s, the idea of traveling to the moon was almost unimaginable. Do you have any great dreams that seem impossible? Does this story make you feel more determined or discouraged? Why?

WHY ON EARTH?

In the 1960s, the United States and the Soviet Union were competing fiercely against each other. Each country wanted to prove that it was the most powerful nation with the best technology and the best scientists. In the early 1960s, the Russians seemed to be winning. They had launched the first satellite to orbit the Earth, and had sent a person to space. In 1961, President John F. Kennedy declared the landing on the moon to be a priority.

DANGER AHEAD!

Getting to the moon was a huge challenge. There's no oxygen, very little gravity, and high amounts of radiation on the lunar surface! But nothing would be more dangerous than the return trip — nobody really knew what would happen.

AS A RESULT ...

The successful moon journey immediately established the United States as the leader in the space race. Many technical innovations created for the Apollo mission became part of our everyday lives — everything from electronic computers to fireproof bedding in hospitals. Some say the most important thing that came out of this amazing journey was the idea that humans can really go anywhere if we put our minds to it.

The crew of Apollo 11 (left to right) Neil Armstrong, Michael Collins, and Buzz Aldrin

Quick Fact

The astronauts left behind many objects on the moon, including lunar vehicles and even their cameras! This was because they couldn't carry too much weight on their return flight to Earth. They had collected many moon rock specimens, which already added to their shuttle's weight.

TO BOLDLY GO WHERE NO ONE HAS GONE BEFORE

These quotations from key people involved in the Apollo project provide insight into the amazing mission to the moon:

"This has been far more than three men on a mission to the moon; more, still, than the efforts of a government and industry team; more, even, than the efforts of one nation. We feel that this stands as a symbol of the insatiable curiosity of all mankind to explore the unknown. Today I feel we're really fully capable of accepting expanded roles in the exploration of space."

— Buzz Aldrin, lunar module pilot on *Apollo 11*

insatiable: *not easily satisfied*

"For every American, this has to be the proudest day of our lives. And for people all over the world, I am sure they too join with Americans in recognizing what an immense feat this is."

— Former President Richard Nixon

"Apollo was a multidimensional success, triumphant not only as a feat of scientific and engineering precision, but also as a demonstration of our country's spirit and competence ... [T]his great adventure transcended nationality and became a milestone for mankind."

— James E. Webb, NASA administrator in the 1960s

transcended: *went beyond*

? Some people claim that the moon landing never happened and that it was a well-staged hoax! Do your own research to find out what their claims are and what evidence they have to support them. What do you think really happened?

The Expert Says ...

"[T]he important achievement of Apollo was a demonstration that humanity is not forever chained to this planet, and our visions go rather further than that, and our opportunities are unlimited.

— Neil Armstrong, commander of *Apollo 11*

On May 25, 1961, former President John F. Kennedy said, "I believe that this nation should commit itself to achieving the goal, before the decade is out, of landing a man on the moon... ."

Take Note

Neil Armstrong and his *Apollo 11* crew went beyond this world, all the way to the moon. Even today, this extraordinary mission is still tops when it comes to space exploration. For these reasons, Neil Armstrong is our #1 pick of boldest explorers on our list.
• What do you imagine could be the next "giant leap" for humankind? Explain.

5   4   3   2   1

We Thought …

Here are the criteria we used in ranking the 10 boldest explorers.

The explorer:
- Visited faraway places
- Ventured into uncharted territory
- Entered forbidden lands
- Traveled long distances
- Went to many different places around the world
- Challenged his or her own abilities
- Overcame obstacles in the environment
- Showed courage and determination
- Was a pioneer
- Changed the course of history

What Do You Think?

1. Do you agree with our ranking? If you don't, try ranking them yourself. Justify your ranking with data from your own research and reasoning. You may refer to our criteria, or you may want to draw up your own list of criteria.

2. Here are three other bold explorers we considered, but in the end did not include in our top 10 list: Herodotus, Zheng He, and Jacques-Yves Cousteau.
   • Find out more about them. Do you think they should have made our list? Give reasons for your response.
   • Are there other explorers who you think should have made our list? Explain your choices.

Index

A
Africa, 7–8, 27, 40
Aldrin, Edwin Buzz, 43–45
Altitude, 10, 13
Amazon, 14–17
Amundsen, Roald, 22–25, 29
Apollo 11, 42–45
Armstrong, Neil, 42–45
Asia, 11–12, 21, 27, 31–32, 39–40
Astronaut, 43–44
Atlantic Ocean, 16, 39

B
Battuta, Abu Abdallah Ibn, 26–29, 33
Beijing, 13
Buddhism, 10, 12, 19–20

C
Cairo, 7
Camels, 7, 9
Cameron, Ian, 41
China, 13, 18–20, 28, 31–32, 41
Circumnavigation, 34–36
Civilization, 8, 28
Columbus, Christopher, 32, 38–41
Collins, Michael, 44

D
Dalai Lama, 12
David-Neel, Alexandra, 10–13, 17
de Orellana, Francisco, 14–17
Desert, 19–21, 32–33, 40
Drake, Francis, 34–37, 41

E
Egypt, 7–8
El Dorado, 16
England, 12, 35–37
Europe, 8, 11–12
Expedition, 16, 23–25, 35

F
Florida, 43
Foster, Barbara, 12

G
Gelman, David, 41
Glacier, 11, 24
Gold, 7–9, 15–16, 40
Golden Hind, 36–37

H
Himalayas, 11–13

I
Il Milione (Travels of Marco Polo), 32–33
India, 12, 19–21, 27, 41
Indian Ocean, 40
Islam, 8
Italy, 31–32, 40

J
Japan, 41

K
Kennedy, John F., 43–45
Kublai Khan, 32, 37
Kunze, Albert F., 16

L
Lhasa, 10–13

M
Magnetism, 24
Mali, 7–9
Mecca, 6–9, 27–29
Mediterranean Sea, 40
Middle East, 27
Middle Kingdom, 30–32
Monk, 17, 19–20
Moon, 42–45
Morocco, 27–28
Mountain, 11–12, 19–20, 40
Musa, Mansa, 6–9, 13, 27

N
Nansen, Fridtjof, 25
NASA, 44–45
Netsilik, 24
New World, 39–41
Nixon, Richard, 44–45
North Pole, 24–25

O
Old World, 39–41

P
Pacific Ocean, 36
Peru, 16
Philosophy, 12, 20
Pilgrimage, 7–9, 28
Pizarro, Gonzalo, 16
Plague, 28
Polar exploration, 24
Polo, Marco, 30–33, 37
Portugal, 40

Q
Queen Elizabeth I, 35–37

R
Ramusio, Giovanni Battista, 33
Rihla, 28–29
Runciman, Walter, 36

S
Sahara, 7–8
Salloum, Habeeb, 8
Saudi Arabia, 7
Scott, Robert F., 23
Scriptures, 19–20
Soldier, 9, 16, 37
South America, 15–16, 35–36

South Pole, 22–25
Soviet Union, 44
Spain, 12, 16, 36, 39
Spanish Empire, 35
Switzerland, 12

T
Territory, 5, 17, 39
Tibet, 10–13
Timbuktu, 8
Translations, 20
Trek, 11, 13, 19

U
United States, 33, 44

V
Venice, 30–32
Viking, 23

W
Warship, 37
Weatherford, Jack, 41
Webb, James E., 45
Wolfe, Michael, 28
Wriggins, Salley Hovey, 21

X
Xuanzang, 18–21, 25

Y
Yongden, Aphur, 11–12